A Note to Parents

DK RE
childre
experts   y Fellow of the
Univer   many years as
a teacher and teacher educator specializing in reading and
has written more than 160 books for children and teachers.
He is series editor to Collins Big Cat.

Beautiful illustrations and superb full-colour photographs
combine with engaging, easy-to-read stories to offer a fresh
approach to each subject in the series. Each DK READER
is guaranteed to capture a child's interest while developing
his or her reading skills, general knowledge, and
love of reading.

The five levels of DK READERS are aimed at different
reading abilities, enabling you to choose the books that
are exactly right for your child:

Pre-level 1: Learning to read
Level 1: Beginning to read
Level 2: Beginning to read alone
Level 3: Reading alone
Level 4: Proficient readers

The "normal" age at which a child
begins to read can be anywhere
from three to eight years old.
Adult participation through the lower
levels is very helpful for providing
encouragement, discussing storylines
and sounding out unfamiliar words.

No matter which level you
select, you can be sure that you
are helping your child learn to
read, then read to learn!

LONDON, NEW YORK, MUNICH,
MELBOURNE, AND DELHI

Series Editor Deborah Lock
Senior Art Editor Sonia Whillock-Moore
Production Editor Siu Chan
Production Pip Tinsley
Jacket Designer Sonia Whillock-Moore
Photographer Andy Crawford
Production Photographer Keith Pattison

Reading Consultant
Cliff Moon, M.Ed.

Published in Great Britain by
Dorling Kindersley Limited
80 Strand, London WC2R ORL

Copyright © 2008 Dorling Kindersley Limited
A Penguin Company

2 4 6 8 10 9 7 5 3 1
DD395 - 12/07

A CIP catalogue record for this book
is available from the British Library

ISBN: 978-1-40532-920-0

Colour reproduction by Colourscan, Singapore
Printed and bound in China by L Rex Printing Co., Ltd.

The publisher wishes to thank Cavan Day-Lewis,
Caroline Day-Lewis and Stewart Cairns.
The production of *Flat Stanley* featured was produced by West
Yorkshire Playhouse and Polka Theatre in 2006-7. Based on the
story by Jeff Brown with illustrations by Scott Nash and adapted for
the stage by Mike Kenny. It was directed by Gail McIntyre, designed
by Karen Tennent, lighting design by Ian Scott, animation by
John Barber, composition by Julian Ronnie and sound design by
Martin Pickersgill. The original cast were Ian Bonar, Stewart
Cairns, Lisa Howard, and Robin Simpson.
Flat Stanley is published by Egmont in the UK
and by HarperCollins in the United States.
With thanks also to all at Polka Theatre, Wimbledon, London,
www.polkatheatre.com, including Chris Barham, James Cartwright,
Anwen Cooper, Hélène Hill, Tim Highman, Paula Hopkins, Anne
James, Kim Kish, Ben Powell-Williams, and Mary Trafford.
Flat Stanley illustration © Scott Nash

The publisher would like to thank the following for their kind
permission to reproduce their photographs:
a=above, b=below/bottom, c=centre, l=left, r=right, t=top
Alamy Images: Frank Chmura 32. **Flickr.com:**
vancouverfringephotos 24-25b. **Kenneth A. Goldberg:** 30t.
All other images © Dorling Kindersley
For more information see: www.dkimages.com

Discover more at
www.dk.com

DK READERS

A Trip to the Theatre

Written by Deborah Lock

A Dorling Kindersley Book

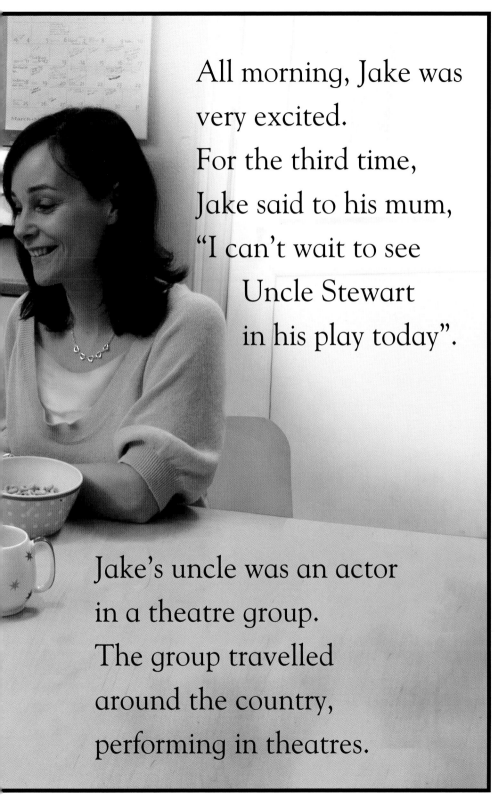

All morning, Jake was
very excited.
For the third time,
Jake said to his mum,
"I can't wait to see
Uncle Stewart
in his play today".

Jake's uncle was an actor
in a theatre group.
The group travelled
around the country,
performing in theatres.

After lunch, Jake and his mum
went to the theatre to meet Stewart.
Stewart was going to take
them on a tour of
the backstage area,
before they watched
the play.

As they arrived,
Jake looked up at
the theatre's large sign.
All around the entrance,
there were posters
that showed the dates and
times of the performances.

Jake eagerly pushed open
the doors and stepped into
the theatre foyer.
His mum went to the box office
to buy two tickets for the play.

Then Stewart came to meet them.
"Hello, Jake," said Stewart
with a beaming smile.
"Welcome to the theatre.
Let me show you around."

"I'll show you the auditorium first,"
said Stewart, leading the way.
"This is where you'll sit to watch
our performance."
"Wow, it's big," Jake gasped,
as he looked at all the seats.
"Yes, there are 300 seats,"
explained Stewart.
"At the back is the control room
where the sound-and-lighting
operator sits during the play."

Stage lighting
Lights shine on to
the actors on stage.
Different shades and
colours help to change
the mood of a play.

"The stage is set up for my favourite scene," said Stewart. "This is the park where my character flies his kite."

"What are the trees, kites and boats made of?" asked Jake. "Just painted wood and paper," said Stewart.
"Let's go backstage and I'll show you where they were made."

Stewart led Jake and
his mum through a door
into the backstage area.
"This is the workshop,"
said Stewart.
"Our props manager, Ben, makes
the scenery and props here."
"What are props?"
asked Jake.
"They are the things
that actors use on
stage," said Stewart.

Fake food

Food props are often
made from foam, clay,
wire mesh or paper,
and then painted to
look real.

"Next, I'll show you where our costumes are made," said Stewart. They entered a room full of colourful clothes, hats and wigs. "This is Sue," said Stewart. "She designs the costumes we wear in our plays."

"Would you like to try on this police officer's costume?" Sue asked Jake. "Yes, please," replied Jake. Jake laughed at his reflection in the mirror.

Costume designer

Costumes are based on sketches drawn by the costume designer. She chooses the styles and fabrics to suit the play.

"Now let's take a look at the area behind the stage," said Stewart. As they walked downstairs, they met James, the director. "Hi, Stewart," said James. "Are you ready for the show? The final rehearsal went really well yesterday." "What's a rehearsal?" asked Jake. "It's a practice performance of the play," explained Stewart.

Director

The director oversees every part of the play. He helps everyone work together to make the show a success.

It was very dark behind the stage.
"This is Chris, the stage manager,"
said Stewart.

"What are you doing?" asked Jake.
"I'm making sure that all the props
and costumes are in the right
places," replied Chris.
"We need to know exactly where
they are so that we
can find them quickly
during the play,"
added Stewart.

Stage manager

The stage manager
makes sure everything is
running smoothly during
the performance, both
onstage and backstage.

21

"In this show, some of the actors play more than one character," explained Chris.
"They have to change quickly from one costume to another."

"The actor who plays the father also plays a doctor, a security guard and a policeman!" Stewart added.

"I'll look out for him in the play," said Jake.

"If we hurry, we'll have time to see the control room," said Stewart.

"Follow me."

23

"This is Abby, the operator," said Stewart, as they entered the control room. "During the performance, she uses the control panel to change the lighting and create sound effects."

"I have to follow the script carefully so I don't miss my cue," said Abby.

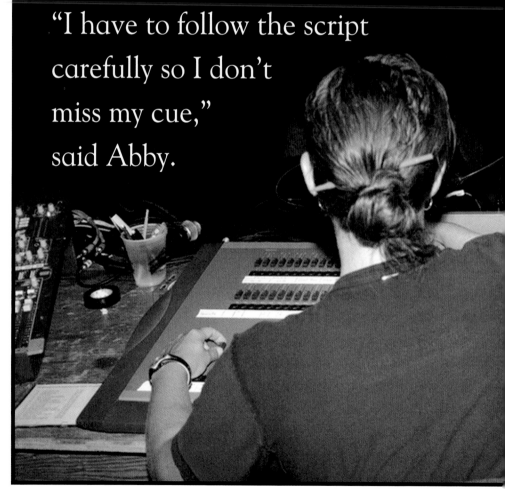

"A cue is a signal, such as a word or an action," explained Stewart.

"Come and see my
dressing room," said Stewart.
They entered a room filled with
mirrors surrounded by bright lights.
"I sit here to put on my make-up,"
said Stewart.

"We should go and find our seats," said Mum. "Good luck, Stewart." "Sometimes people say 'break a leg' instead of 'good luck' to actors before a show," explained Stewart. "Break a leg," laughed Jake.

"Now it's time to get into character," thought Stewart. He started to put on his make-up.

"I think I need more colour on my chin," he said.

Next, he painted his lips
and cheeks a rosy red
and added black freckles
with a thin paintbrush.
Finally, Stewart pinned
on his orange wig.
"Perfect!" he said.
He put on his costume
and headed off to the stage.

Meanwhile, Jake and his mum were sitting in the auditorium, surrounded by chattering people. Suddenly, the lights faded, the audience stopped talking, and the music began. The play was about the adventures of a boy, who was played by Stewart.

Mum bought Jake an ice-cream
during the interval.
In the second half, Stewart's
character caught a burglar.
It was very exciting.
At the end, the actors
bowed to the audience and
Jake clapped very loudly.
"That was fantastic!" he said.

THE END

SCOTTISH BORDERS COUNCIL
LIBRARY &

Theatre Facts

The ancient Greeks performed their plays in large outdoor theatres called amphitheatres. The actors wore masks to represent their characters.

Medieval plays were first performed on wagons in large outdoor marketplaces.

Later, open-air playhouses were built. Audiences sat or stood on three sides of the stage. Hardly any scenery was used.

During the 17th and 18th centuries, plays were performed in fully lit rooms. The stage had a decorative frame around it.

Today, audiences sit in the dark, watching the performance on a lit stage. Plays may have lots of scenery and special effects. Some famous plays are made into films.